Searchlight BOOKS™

What-If Science?

Could We Tame a Tornado?

Cynthia O'Brien

Lerner Publications ◆ Minneapolis

Lerner Publications Company
An imprint of Lerner Publishing Group, Inc.
241 First Avenue North
Minneapolis, MN 55401 USA

For reading levels and more information, look up this title at www.lernerbooks.com.

Main body text set in Adrianna Regular.
Typeface provided by Chank.

Library of Congress Cataloging-in-Publication Data

Names: O'Brien, Cynthia (Cynthia J.) author
Title: Could we tame a tornado? / Cynthia O'Brien.
Description: Minneapolis : Lerner Publications, [2026] | Series: Searchlight books. What-if science? | Includes bibliographical references and index. | Audience: Ages 8–11 | Audience: Grades 4–6 | Summary: "Multiple theories for taming tornadoes exist, but none have worked yet. Discover the science of tornadoes, and different ways we might be able to stop them"—Provided by publisher.
Identifiers: LCCN 2025013515 (print) | LCCN 2025013516 (ebook) | ISBN 9798765688953 lib. bdg. | ISBN 9798348029159 pbk | ISBN 9798765698020 epub
Subjects: LCSH: Tornadoes—Juvenile literature | Weather control—Juvenile literature
Classification: LCC QC955.2 .O27 2026 (print) | LCC QC955.2 (ebook) | DDC 551.68/53—dc23/eng/20250716

LC record available at https://lccn.loc.gov/2025013515
LC ebook record available at https://lccn.loc.gov/2025013516

Manufactured in the United States of America
1 – CG – 12/15/25

Table of Contents

Chapter 1

TERRIBLE TWISTERS

A violent tornado hit Ellington, Missouri, at about one o'clock in the afternoon on March 18, 1925. For the next three and a half hours, the twister whipped across 219 miles (352 km). It roared through Missouri, Illinois, and Indiana and destroyed everything in its path. When the storm finally stopped, 695 people had died. Over two thousand people were injured. Thousands of people were left homeless. The Tri-State Tornado is still the deadliest tornado in American history.

In 1925, there were no tornado warnings. Now, meteorologists know much more about tornadoes. So far, there is no way to stop tornadoes. But people have ideas for how to stop them. And tornado watches and warnings can help people prepare for them.

The Tri-State Tornado destroyed homes, schools, and farms.

What is a Tornado?

A tornado is made of a spinning column of air called a vortex. The vortex stretches from high in the storm clouds to the ground. Tornado winds spin at speeds of up to 300 miles (483 km) per hour. Tornadoes can last for a few seconds to more than an hour. Most tornadoes exist for around ten minutes.

A tornado is a twisting tube of air.

Where Tornadoes Happen

Tornadoes happen in most parts of the world, except Antarctica. The United States has the most tornadoes, with around 1,200 each year. Canada has about ninety-seven tornadoes per year. The worst tornado in history happened in 1989 in Bangladesh, in South Asia. The tornado killed about 1,300 people and injured twelve thousand. It destroyed more than twenty villages.

The powerful tornado in Bangladesh tore down houses.

Tornado Ratings

Since 2007, tornadoes have been rated on the Enhanced Fujita Scale. This scale looks at wind speeds and the damage the tornado has caused. The scale rates tornadoes from zero, for the weakest, to five, for the strongest. The most violent tornadoes are strong enough to rip up trees and tear houses apart. They can toss heavy objects, such as cars and trucks, into the air. Flying debris and broken glass can injure people and animals.

A tornado with a score of four to five on the Enhanced Fujita Scale

Deep Dive

Tornado Alley

Tornado Alley is a nickname for an area of the United States where many tornadoes happen. It includes flat grasslands of Texas, Oklahoma, Kansas, the Dakotas, and Nebraska. Here, cool, dry air from the north meets warm, humid air from the south. This mixture helps tornadoes to form. Tornadoes usually happen here in late spring and summer. However, tornadoes also occur in all other states and can happen at any time of the year.

Tornado damage in Dallas, Texas

Chapter 2

SPINNING INTO DISASTER

Most tornadoes come from supercell storms. Supercells are severe thunderstorms. They contain a wide, rotating column of air. Supercells form when warm, humid air rises quickly into very cold, dry air. This can create a tall storm cloud.

Inside the cloud, wind whirls around in different directions. This causes the updraft, the rising current of air, to spin at high speed. A supercell storm can last for hours. It might produce rain, lightning, and large ice pellets called hail. Sometimes, a supercell releases part of its energy in a tornado.

SUPERCELL STORMS ARE LARGE THUNDERSTORMS WITH ROTATING WINDS.

A funnel cloud is made of water droplets.

A Tornado Forms

Why do some supercells produce a tornado and others do not? A supercell may produce a funnel cloud and not a tornado. A funnel cloud is a spinning tunnel of air. It looks like a tornado, but it does not touch the ground. People can see this column of air even though wind is invisible. This is because the wind contains water droplets, dust, and debris. If the funnel cloud connects with the ground, it becomes a tornado.

Supercells may produce one violent tornado or a few tornadoes. A multi-vortex tornado is a storm with two or more spinning columns inside the main vortex. A separate tornado sometimes forms during the same storm. If a storm produces two or more tornadoes, it is called a tornado family.

THESE TORNADOES CAME FROM THE SAME SUPERCELL STORM.

Shapes and Sizes

Tornadoes come in different sizes and shapes. Large, wedge-shaped tornadoes can be 2 miles (3.2 km) across. These tornadoes look as wide as they are tall. Other tornadoes may be shaped like an ice cream cone, a rope, or an elephant's trunk. A tornado may be small but still cause a lot of damage.

A swirling tornado over Texas

LANDSPOUTS FORM FROM THE GROUND UP AND HAVE A NARROW FUNNEL.

Different Tornadoes

Other kinds of thunderstorms can produce tornadoes. They are usually smaller and weaker than tornadoes produced by supercells. Landspouts can happen when a thunderstorm is still growing. They form from spinning air near the ground. Landspouts usually only last a few minutes.

Waterspouts are tornadoes that happen over warm water. They often come from a thunderstorm and strong winds. Fair-weather waterspouts do not need a storm to form. These tornadoes start to swirl on the surface of the water and spin upwards. Waterspouts can damage boats. If a waterspout moves onto land, it can cause damage there.

Waterspouts can form over water or move from land to water.

A fire tornado burns trees in Colorado.

Fire Tornadoes

The heat from a wildfire can spark a storm and tornado. This happened in California in 2018. A vortex of smoke, ash, and fire rose about 17,000 feet (5,182 m) into the air. Fire tornadoes are very rare. Fire whirls are much smaller and more common. They are usually about 33 to 100 feet (10 to 30 m) high. Fire tornadoes and fire whirls can cause a lot of damage.

Deep Dive
Twisting Winds

Wind shear is key to tornadoes forming. It is wind blowing in different speeds and directions at different heights. Speed shear is measured by the speed of the wind as it goes up. This tilts the supercell. Directional shear is the wind changing directions. This causes the supercell to rotate.

Wind shear is the changes in wind speed and direction.

Chapter 3

TORNADO WATCH

Tornadoes are hard to predict. Most storms do not produce tornadoes at all. Tornadoes can change direction. Sometimes they stay in one spot. They may return to the same area or spin across long distances.

Tornado Technology

Doppler radar is an important tool for gathering information about tornadoes. There are about 160 radar stations across the United States. The radar sends out and receives signals about wind speed, direction, and precipitation. The information is fed to computers that put it all together.

Scientists at a weather station

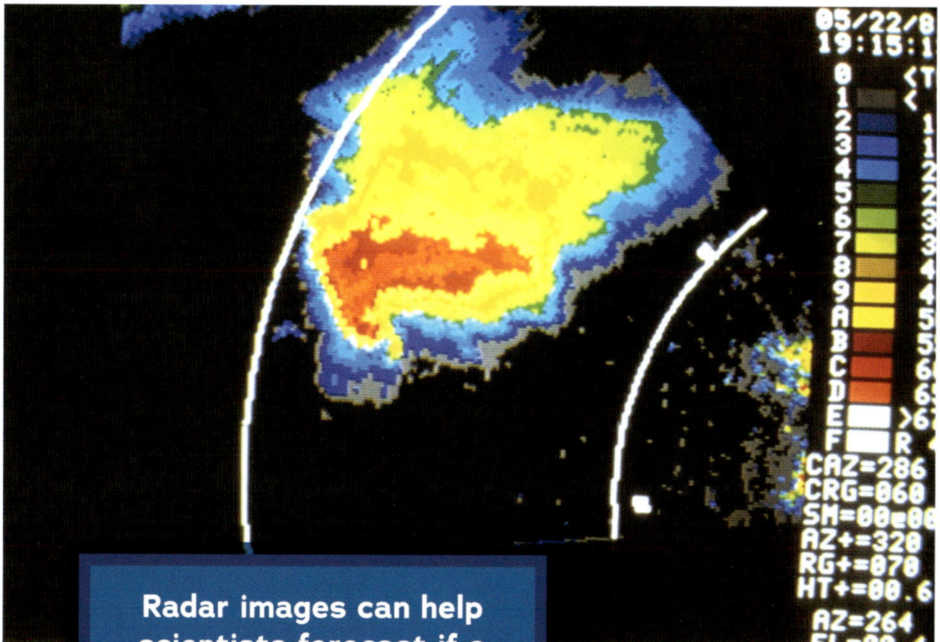

Radar images can help scientists forecast if a tornado is going to form.

Doppler radar helps to spot tornadoes by detecting wind rotation. It finds out how raindrops in the storm are moving. If the rotation of the vortex is strong enough, the computer shows this as the Tornado Vortex Signature (TVS). A TVS does not mean that a tornado will form, but it gives scientists a clue. Thunderstorms can cover a large area. The TVS gives scientists a better idea of exactly where a tornado might develop. The latest radar technology is Phased Array Radar. This can scan the sky and update information in under a minute.

Storm spotters are people who are trained to watch for tornadoes. They look for thunderclouds and check the wind speed. Spotters see a storm forming in real time. They can send up-to-date information to their local weather station.

Storm spotters are volunteers who look for tornadoes.

Watch Out!

A tornado watch means a tornado may happen. People should be on alert. If a tornado is expected, or has been seen, there is a tornado warning. This means that people must move to safety. If possible, they should go to the basement of a sturdy building. They should stay away from windows. Warnings may only come about fifteen or twenty minutes before a tornado hits. A tornado emergency is the highest alert level. This means that a severe tornado is happening. People must get to a safe place right away.

Tornado safe rooms are made to stand up to strong winds.

Spotlight On:
National Severe Storms Laboratory

Top meteorologists and engineers work at the National Severe Storms Laboratory (NSSL) in the United States. They study tornadoes and other serious storms inside and outside the lab. NSSL work with National Weather Service stations across the country. They use the latest computers and radar technology. New and better ways to understand storms help the NSSL to predict tornadoes more quickly.

An NSSL radar dome

Stopping the Spin

Strong thunderstorms and tornadoes need the right conditions to keep going. This includes warm, humid air and wind shear. If things change, the storm can weaken. What if people could make the air cooler or change the wind's direction? Could they prevent a tornado from forming?

PEOPLE HAVE DIFFERENT IDEAS ABOUT HOW WE COULD STOP A TORNADO.

Cloud seeding is one idea. This drops chemicals into clouds to create rain and cool the air. Other chemicals might soak up water in the humid air. Drones would have to throw these chemicals into the tornado. But the tornado would most likely destroy the drones before they could get close enough. Also, it would be impossible to throw enough chemicals into the tornado and to get them in the right place. Even if this was possible, the thunderstorm could just produce another tornado.

Some countries use cloud seeding to make rain or snow.

Another idea is to explode a tornado with a bomb. The bomb would need to be very powerful to attack the energy in a thunderstorm. This would be very dangerous. The bomb's explosion would cause a lot more damage than the tornado.

Ideas like these make for exciting stories and movies, but scientists say they will not work. Also, they disturb natural weather patterns. Tornadoes are just a small part of a much larger system. Thunderstorms are full of energy. They keep Earth's energy in balance and direct it back to the ground.

The damage from a bomb could be worse than from a tornado (*below*).

Climate Change

Climate change is the change in Earth's temperature and weather over a long time. Earth is heating up and extreme weather, such as supercell storms, is more common. No one knows if climate change will bring more tornadoes overall. However, tornadoes are happening more often in winter and in areas that did not have tornadoes before. Understanding tornadoes is important. More accurate tornado forecasts will protect property and keep people safe. The more we find out about these twisting storms, the better prepared we can be.

Climate change is making floods happen more often.

But What If We Did?

Taming a tornado could be a good thing. People would not have to worry about losing their homes or getting hurt. But what methods would work and be safe to use? A bomb would cause more damage than the tornado. If we used chemicals, could we inject enough of them, and would they harm the environment? What happens to the land and wildlife if we stop tornadoes spreading seeds, clearing land, and bringing rain?

Glossary

debris: pieces of things that have been destroyed

drone: a flying device that is controlled from the ground

humid: containing a lot of water vapor

meteorologist: a scientist who studies weather

precipitation: rain, snow, sleet, or hail

predict: tell that something will happen

rotating: turning around a center point

satellite: a spacecraft in space that sends information to Earth

tornado: a violent, spinning column of air that stretches from a storm cloud to the ground; also called a twister

updraft: an upward movement of air

Learn More

Abramson, Marcia. *Tornadoes*. Bearport Publishing Company, 2024.

American Museum of Natural History: Tornadoes: Spinning Thunderstorms
https://www.amnh.org/explore/ology/earth/tornadoes-spinning-thunderstorms#:~:text=If%20a%20storm%20is%20strong,to%20rip%20up%20the%20earth.

CBC Kids News: Watch: Tornadoes Explained
https://www.cbc.ca/kidsnews/post/watch-tornadoes-explained-how-they-form-and-what-to-look-out-for

Crane, Cody. *All About Tornadoes*. Children's Press, 2021.

National Geographic Kids: Tornadoes
https://kids.nationalgeographic.com/science/article/tornado

O'Brien, Cynthia. *Could We Harness the Power of Black Holes?* Lerner Publications, 2026.

Index

Photo Acknowledgments

Image credits: Science History Images/Alamy, p. 5; Minverva Studio/Shutterstock, p. 6; Associated Press/Alamy, p. 7; aapsky/Shutterstock, p. 8; Walker Photography/Shutterstock, p. 9; Minderva Studio/Shutterstock, p. 11; NOAA Photo Library, p. 12; Huntstyle/Shutterstock, p.13; Wirestock/iStock, p. 14; Stefan Klein/Alamy, p, 15; Koto_feja/iStock, p. 16; milehightraveler/iStock, p. 17; EyeEm Mobile GmbH/iStock, p. 18; Dennis MacDonald/Shutterstock, p. 20; OAR/ERL/National Severe Storms Laboratory/NOAA Photo Library, p. 21; Peopleimages/iStock, p. 22; SShepard/iStock, p. 23; dvande/Shutterstock, p. 24; OAR/ERL/National Severe Storms Laboratory/NOAA Photo Library, p. 25; Arnold O.A. Pinto/Shutterstock, p. 26; Gregory Simpson/Shutterstock, p. 27; TLF/Shutterstock, p. 28.

Cover: solarseven/Shutterstock.